SEED Pack 1

PRISCILLA SHIRER

forgotten **01**

enough **02**

control **03**

LifeWay
Biblical Solutions for Life

SEED Pack 1

Priscilla Shirer

LifeWay Press®
Nashville, Tennessee

Published by LifeWay Press®
© 2011 Priscilla Shirer
Second printing 2011

ISBN 978-1-4158-6958-1
Item 005342725

Dewey decimal classification: 248.84
Subject Headings: TRUST \ LONELINESS \ PROVIDENCE AND GOVERNMENT OF GOD

To order additional copies of this resource, write to LifeWay Church Resources Customer Service; One LifeWay Plaza, Nashville, TN 37234-0013; fax (615) 251-5933; call toll free (800) 458-2772; e-mail orderentry@lifeway.com; order online at www. lifeway.com; or visit the LifeWay Christian Store serving you.

Published in the United States of America

Leadership and Adult Publishing
LifeWay Church Resources
One LIfeWay Plaza
Nashville, TN 37234-0175

contents

about the author

PRISCILLA SHIRER is a wife and mom first but put a Bible in her hand and a message in her heart and you'll see why thousands meet God in powerful, personal ways through her resources and conferences. Through the expository teaching of God's Word, Priscilla's desire is to see women not only know the uncompromising truths of Scripture intellectually but also to experience them practically by the power of the Holy Spirit.

Priscilla is a graduate of Dallas Theological Seminary and the author of several books and Bible studies including *A Jewel In His Crown, Discerning the Voice of God,* and *One in a Million.* She and her husband, Jerry, lead Going Beyond Ministries from their hometown of Dallas, Texas, never too far from their three growing boys.

www.goingbeyond.com

WAIT!
Don't turn the page yet.
I've gotta talk to you first.

I'm so glad you're joining me. I love Bible study. Anyone who knows me can attest to that. Since you have this book in your hand, I'm assuming you love it too. Yet I've often wondered if, in our desire to dig deeply into the treasure of God's Word, we may be missing one of the most critical and stunning realities of our relationship with the Bible: God speaks not only to shape our theology but to mold our current reality.

You see, I'll admit that I'm hooked on theology. The mere sight of a bookshelf filled with Bible commentaries makes my breath catch. Yet amidst the commentaries, Bible research software, and scholarly data that I would always encourage you to benefit from, God's own Spirit began to whisper sweetly to me, asking me to come to Him with nothing open except His Word and my heart, ready to hear His voice and to experience the living, active power of the Scriptures. Armed with this new objective, God prompted me to make certain my devotional time was as rich as my Bible study time.

To be clear: I'm not suggesting that we disregard the amazing resources we've been offered to help us rightly divide the Word of truth. I'm only suggesting that we not neglect the powerful experience of meditating on God's Word in the process. If you have felt the same stirring, we have designed this resource to assist.

Prepare yourself, my friend. This resource will most likely be different from the last study you had in your hands. You won't find mounds of documented insights or words researched in their original form for meaning. Nor have I provided the amount of application questions you'd normally expect from something I'd write. While I've occasionally included some help and worked hard to be certain we use passages in context, I purposely designed this study to lead you back to personal meditation, prayerful observation, and listening to God's Spirit as He seeks to illumine Scripture.

If you feel a bit of hesitation (that maybe you should grab your receipt and head back to the bookstore rather than grab a pen), I urge you to turn the first page and dive in. Any reluctance you feel is understandable. In our highly blessed culture where we have Bible study resources at our immediate disposal, we've become a bit handicapped and ... can I say it ... lazy. We like the work being done by someone more "capable," more "spiritual," more ... ahhh, you fill in the blank. But you, my friend, are filled with God's Spirit. He is ready to be your personal tour guide through the Word. So don't quit before you've even started. I think you will be surprised with the outcome.

How this resource works

At the beginning of each week you'll read an article and watch a video session, if you've decided to get the video. You can use this workbook without the video. Both the article and video will present a theme for you to consider before the Lord for the remainder of that week. Then each week I've given you Scripture to consider that complements the theme. You will notice that we've given you 10 passages per subject. Choose one daily, and give it your attention. If you do one per day, you could start the study all over again and have more verses to study on the same themes.

I'm asking you to use the following principles in your devotional time. I call them the "Five P's of Hearing God Through the Bible." They have revolutionized my quiet time, and I'm excited to share them with you. When you've chosen the passage you want to concentrate on, apply these principles.

The Five P's

1. Position Yourself to Hear from God
Engage in solitude and silence, and approach the text with anticipation, expecting God to speak to you.

2. Pore Over the Passage and Paraphrase the Major Points
Don't just skim the passage. Take your time and meditate on it (Josh. 1:8). Read the passage a few times, emphasizing different words in the verse each time. If a certain word or phrase speaks to you, don't ignore it. Stop and consider why it is meaningful. This is how the Spirit speaks. He connects Scripture to the details of our lives.

If the passage allows, put yourself in the Scripture and see yourself in the story. If one verse seems to resonate with you, don't worry about finishing the rest—just stay in the passage, and let the Spirit speak to you. As you meditate on Scripture, consider the context. What takes place both before and after the passage?

After you've meditated on the verse(s), use the space we've given you to paraphrase each verse. In just one or two simple sentences, summarize what is happening. These questions might help you to get the most out of each verse selection as you pore over the passage:

- Who are the major participants?
- What are they doing? saying?
- Where are they going?

3. Pull Out the Spiritual Principles
Close your Bible and look at your paraphrases. For each one spiritualize the major point. What is God teaching? What is He revealing about Himself? Is there a command to be followed? Is there a promise to be regarded? Write them down.

4. Pose the Question

Turn each spiritual principle that you listed above into a personally directed question. Ask yourself questions that will help you come to these conclusions:

- Am I living in a way that coincides with the message of this verse?
- Is anything in my life contradicting this passage?
- What do I need to do to bring my life in line with this verse?

As you sit in God's presence with these questions, record what you begin to hear the Spirit encouraging you, convicting you, challenging you, or inspiring you to do.

5. Plan Obedience and Pin Down a Date

Determine the steps you can take to immediately begin responding to what God has said to you, and put them into practice immediately. If obedience requires you to do something specific, record a date and time you will follow through. Let someone else know about your plan so you can be held accountable.

A Personal Example

Here's an illustration from my personal journal from several years ago on how these principles assisted me to have a meaningful conversation with God. I was reading John 1:36-37. "[John the Baptist] looked at Jesus as He walked, and said, 'Behold, the Lamb of God!' The two disciples heard him speak, and they followed Jesus" (NASB).

After positioning myself to hear from God—the first P—and having nothing but my Bible, journal, and hot cup of tea nearby, I continued with the remaining 4 P's.

Pore and Paraphrase
- Verse 36: John's eyes were on Jesus. John's ministry was focused on pointing out the Lamb of God.

- Verse 37: John's message resulted in an increased desire in the listeners to follow hard after Jesus.

Pull
- Verse 36: True ministry means the minister's eyes are focused on Jesus. True ministry should call all attention only to the Lamb of God.

- Verse 37: True ministry should encourage those who hear to desire an intimate personal experience with Jesus more than a relationship with the minister.

Pose
- Verse 36: Are my eyes focused on Jesus or some-one/something else? If so, what? Do I seek to call attention only to the Lamb of God, or do I seek any for myself?

- Verse 37: When people hear my message, do they want more of me or are they encouraged to seek hard after Him?

Purpose and Pin

· When I teach Bible study and in ministry from this day forward, I must develop messages that focus the listener only on seeing Jesus.

· How can I tweak my message to reflect this goal?

· My intention should not be to call attention to myself in any way.

· I want to begin to see people's interest stirred to experience more of God and less of me after hearing me speak.

On this day I was stunned as the searchlight of God's personal Word to me profoundly penetrated my heart. With His conviction through these two simple verses, the Spirit began redirecting the course of my entire ministry. I am a testament to the fact that God speaks through His Word and what He will say can indeed change the course of your very life.

I have no doubt that if you will utilize the "5 P's" you will marvel at the clarity with which you will begin to hear God. He's ready to speak if we'll just tune in to listen! I don't want to miss one word He has to say, and I'm certain that neither do you.

Are you ready?
Let's go.

Priscilla

SESSION 1

THE SECRET SEER

DVD SESSION: FORGOTTEN

> **"Your Father who sees what is done in secret will reward you."**
> —Matthew 6:4, NASB

Only 8 a.m. and I already felt exhausted. I rolled over on my soft pillow and squinted—my eyes trying to focus on the bright sun-split sky that peeked through the slivers in the shades. Was it morning already?

I groaned and covered my face with a blanket. I felt spent. Energy totally depleted. Felt like I'd gotten in bed only moments ago.

Hmmm. I had.

The evening before we'd tucked our boys into their beds at their normal bedtimes. Everyone had fallen asleep soundly. I jumped into bed shortly after in hopes of a full night of rest. But that wouldn't be. Jude, who was one year old at the time, awoke shortly after midnight. He belted out a scream that could have waked the neighborhood. I raced in to check on him but quickly found that there was nothing wrong. He was just ... up.

Surely a few moments of rocking would put him at ease and back to sleep.

I rocked. I sang. I swayed. I patted. I purred. I rubbed. I paced.

Those moments turned to half-hours. Half hours turned into full ones, four to be exact. These were hours I didn't care to visit. You know them, the wee ones—dark, quiet, still, lonely. I paced the floor, trying to keep the others from waking. Those were isolating, lonesome moments. No one patted me on the back for encouragement. No one cheered me on to the finish. No one observed and applauded my faithful mothering.

Just me and him in the unseen, unnoticed midnight hours. We finally tumbled into bed together at 4 a.m.—baby tucked in the crook of my elbow.

Eventually, he dozed ... eventually.

Unnoticed giving. Giving in secret. Expending extra time, extra energy, extra resources, extra emotional concern— essentially everything with little notice from others. It can all seem so unappreciated sometimes, can't it? So unnoticed. So undervalued.

Yes, I know. It might have seemed so that forlorn night if God's Spirit hadn't had something to say about it.

"Priscilla, I'm the Secret Seer," He whispered just as I began to doze off. "The unnoticed gifts you give are in My full view, and I take pleasure in dispensing reward."

What's the secret gift you've been giving away?

Maybe you've not paced the floor in the wee hours with a wee one lately, but you've been giving, haven't you? That final detail you made certain was finished, the financial gift you slid under the door, the prayer you lifted up for another, the want you sacrificed to meet someone else's need. You've been the unnamed, secret soldier who's marched in and left footprints of love on the landscape of someone's life.

Have you wondered if it's worth it when you walk away and no one says "Thank you"? Have you questioned the energy it required when you come back home feeling a bit spent? Have you wanted to take it back when those invested hours seemed to yield little dividends?

I have good news for you, weary secret giver: There is a Secret Seer. Oh yes, Someone sees, and He is not a mere human whose accolades would dissipate as easily as the curling smoke that appears at the meeting of warm breath with cold air. This One gives grand, vast, and eternal gifts.

Take courage, secret soldier. He saw the good deed, the extended hand, the opened heart, the generous act that you thought had gone unnoted and unobserved.

That which you've depleted He will return—pressed down, shaken together, and running over.

In fact, it seems that knowing gifts like these are offered to secret givers should not only cause us to rest easy in what we've already done but to look for opportunities to do it again and again. Knowing the Secret Seer prompts us to give undercover. To share unnamed. To offer without notice.

Secret servants seem to have a special place in the heart of the Servant Savior.

If you feel unnoticed, unappreciated, and overlooked, just lift up your eyes, and your gaze will fall on the eyes of the Holy One. He is watching every opportunity you've grasped, every gift you've offered, every undisclosed detail you've set straight. He has taken note and promises a reward—one that surpasses mere human attention and applause—the only reward worth receiving anyway.

As you begin to ponder this theme in light of Scripture, notice opposite each passage the reminder to use the 5 P's. We've given you lots of space to record the way the Lord leads you to:

- position yourself to hear from God
- pore over and paraphrase the major points
- pull out the spiritual principles
- pose the questions to consider
- plan obedience and pin down a date

Until the method becomes second nature, continue to review the instructions on pages 7-11. Also, remember that I've provided more Scripture than I expect you to concentrate on this week. Just commit to choose one passage per day and spend adequate time in conversation with God about it. I'm praying for God's blessings for you as you develop the skill of approaching God's Word specifically to hear His voice.

MATTHEW 6:1-4 (NLT)

"Watch out! Don't do your good deeds publicly, to be admired by others, for you will lose the reward from your Father in heaven. When you give to someone in need, don't do as the hypocrites do—blowing trumpets in the synagogues and streets to call attention to their acts of charity! I tell you the truth, they have received all the reward they will ever get. But when you give to someone in need, don't let your left hand know what your right hand is doing. Give your gifts in private, and your Father, who sees everything, will reward you."

"Blowing trumpets in the synagogues" carries the idea of our modern phrase "to blow your own horn." It means to draw attention to oneself.

How easy to fall prey to the "martyr syndrome"—doing things for others but only after being certain they know how much work or expense was required for you to do it.

Do you ever see this dynamic evident in your life? What are some practical ways you can remind yourself to steer clear of this behavior?

Compare and contrast the message of this passage with Matthew 5:16.

JOHN 7:3-5,8-9 (NASB)

At the time when the Jews gathered for the Festival of Tabernacles

"Therefore His brothers said to Him, 'Leave here and go into Judea, so that Your disciples also may see Your works which You are doing. For no one does anything in secret when he himself seeks to be known publicly. If You do these things, show Yourself to the world.' For not even His brothers were believing in Him. ... 'Go up to the feast yourselves; I do not go up to this feast because My time has not yet fully come.' Having said these things to them, He stayed in Galilee."

The feast of Tabernacles was "one of the three feasts that all male Jews were required to attend annually (Deut. 16:16)."[1]

EXODUS 1:16-17,20-21 (NASB)

Pharaoh to the Hebrew midwives

"And he said, 'When you are helping the Hebrew women to give birth and see them upon the birthstool, if it is a son, then you shall put him to death; but if it is a daughter, then she shall live.' But the midwives feared God, and did not do as the king of Egypt had commanded them, but let the boys live. ... So God was good to the midwives, and the people multiplied and became very mighty. Because the midwives feared God, He established households for them."

MATTHEW 23:11–12 (NASB)

Jesus to His disciples

"But the greatest among you shall be your servant.
Whoever exalts himself shall be humbled; and
whoever humbles himself shall be exalted."

position

pore & paraphrase

pull

pose

plan

A derivative of the word humble appears twice in verse 12. In the first case, "humbled" is in the passive voice, signifying that the subject is being acted on; he is the recipient of the act. It means he will be humbled by another.

On the second occasion "humbles" appears in the active voice and indicative mood. Active signifies that the subject is performing the act of humbling himself.

ISAIAH 49:2-4 (NLT)

*God's servant speaking of the small return he saw
for the time and energy invested in ministering*

"He made my words of judgment as sharp as a sword. He has hidden me in the shadow of his hand. I am like a sharp arrow in his quiver. He said to me, 'You are my servant, Israel, and you will bring me glory.' I replied, 'But my work seems so useless! I have spent my strength for nothing and to no purpose. Yet I leave it all in the LORD's hand; I will trust God for my reward.'"

position

pore & paraphrase

pull

pose

plan

For what service are you currently seeing little rewards? Do you feel discouraged? If not, what keeps you encouraged to continue?

JOHN 17:4 (HCSB)

Jesus speaking to the Heavenly Father

"I have glorified You on the earth

by completing the work You gave Me to do."

The work the Father gave Jesus to do included not only the performing of miracles but also loneliness, exhaustive service, and great suffering. List some of the portions of your current circumstances that you'd rather avoid but will commit to in order to complete the work you've been given by the Father.

MATTHEW 25:34-40 (HCSB)

"Then the King will say to those on His right, 'Come, you who are blessed by My Father, inherit the kingdom prepared for you from the foundation of the world. For I was hungry and you gave Me something to eat; I was thirsty and you gave Me something to drink; I was a stranger and you took Me in; I was naked and you clothed Me; I was sick and you took care of Me; I was in prison and you visited Me.' Then the righteous will answer Him, 'Lord, when did we see You hungry and feed You, or thirsty and give You something to drink? When did we see You a stranger and take You in, or without clothes and clothe You? When did we see You sick, or in prison, and visit You?' And the King will answer them, 'I assure you: Whatever you did for one of the least of these brothers of Mine, you did for Me.' "

position

pore & paraphrase

pull

pose

plan

Who are some of the "least of these" in your sphere of influence?

1 CORINTHIANS 15:58 (AMP)

Paul's encouragement to the Corinthian believers

"Therefore, my beloved brethren, be firm (steadfast), immovable, always abounding in the work of the Lord [always being superior, excelling, doing more than enough in the service of the Lord], knowing and being continually aware that your labor in the Lord is not futile [it is never wasted or to no purpose]."

position

pore & paraphrase

pull

pose

plan

Paul gave this charge after a lengthy lesson on the believer's glorified body to be received after life on earth. His premise? Knowing what the future holds should compel us to be that much more diligent in the present.

1 SAMUEL 16:7 (NASB)

During Samuel's search for a king for Israel

"But the LORD said to Samuel, 'Do not look at his
appearance or at the height of his stature, because I have
rejected him; for God sees not as man sees,
for man looks at the outward appearance,
but the LORD looks at the heart.' "

LUKE 12:2-3 (ESV)

Jesus' warning regarding hypocrisy to His disciples

"Nothing is covered up that will not be revealed,

or hidden that will not be known. Therefore whatever

you have said in the dark shall be heard in the light, and

what you have whispered in private rooms shall

be proclaimed on the housetops."

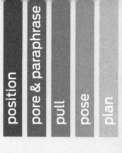

position

pore & paraphrase

pull

pose

plan

The word hypocrite *comes from a Greek word that means "an actor, one who plays a part." Consider this in light of today's passage.*

Both negative and positive activities and intentions will be exposed and uncovered.

MORE SEEDS

Matthew 6:5-6,17-18; Galatians 4:11; 6:9-10; Colossians 3:17; 2 Thessalonians 3:13; Hebrews 6:10; 12:2; 13:16; Job 34:21; Psalms 11:4; 33:13-15; 38:9; 44:21; 139:1-3; Proverbs 5:21; 15:3; Jeremiah 32:19; Proverbs 24:12; Isaiah 45:3; Jeremiah 32:19; 1 Corinthians 4:5

THE 300

> "And the LORD said to Gideon, 'I will deliver you with the 300.'"
> —Judges 7:7, NASB

In the mid-fifth century before Christ a tiny Greek army led by King Leonidas and 300 Spartan warriors fought an invading Persian army estimated between 80,000 and 290,000 men. In a slender canyon at the battle of Thermopylae the Greeks held the huge Persian force at bay for seven days until they were betrayed by a Greek traitor.

Centuries later the idea of so few soldiers holding their own against a vast, military kingdom captured the attention of Hollywood. The result was a multi-million dollar visual extravaganza that had moviegoers glued to the screen.

We're captivated when someone does the seemingly impossible. We love it when the underdog comes out on top. When we learn of their stories, we somehow take on a bit of their strength and own some of their courage. We gird ourselves in their armor, take up their bow, and suddenly feel that a bit of their victory has become our own.

King Leonidas wasn't the first leader of 300. The other 300 were the originals. Hollywood hasn't come knocking for their story. Maybe we have a bit more trouble visualizing it, but the account is brilliantly recorded in the Book of Judges.

Gideon, the commander-in-chief, led a vast army of Israelites. Their ranks initially numbered more than 30,000 and were chomping at the bit to slay the Midianites. Then God dwindled Gideon's army down—not once, but twice.

God didn't pare the army down by a small amount. This reduction in force numbered in the thousands. First God cut the army from more than thirty thousand to ten thousand. Then from ten thousand the army dropped to just a few hundred—three to be exact.

Imagine how Gideon's eyes widened with surprise. Picture the beads of sweat forming on his brow. Hear his loud heartbeat quicken and pound in his chest. Imagine his nerves teetering on the emotional edge. Envision the barrage of questions swimming around in his head. Yet Gideon went to war with these remaining 300 because in the end, these forces were like no other grouping of soldiers.

This was God's 300.

With this small yet divinely ordained group, Gideon forged ahead and claimed a victory. Who knew so much could be accomplished with so little?

Are you running on empty?

Are you tired? Have your circumstances diminished your resources? Are you looking at what remains and wondering how you have any chance of doing so much with so little? Hear the words of our Lord to you, valiant warrior: "I will deliver you with the 300."

Your 300 seem so few, don't they? What you have seems so little, especially when you face such obstacles and must climb mountainous circumstances.

Here's the secret: You're better off with God's 300 than your own 30,000 because His deliverance is only guaranteed to come through His supply. Bigger isn't always better. More is vastly overrated. Believe it or not, you have exactly what you need in time, gifts, talents, provision, and spiritual resources. In fact, He has graciously "granted to [you] everything pertaining to life and godliness" (2 Pet. 1:3, NASB).

Everything.

So, onward soldier. It's the 300.

It's God's 300.

And it's enough.

EXODUS 4:10-13 (NLT)

"But Moses pleaded with the LORD, 'O LORD, I'm not very good with words. I never have been, and I'm not now, even though you have spoken to me. I get tongue-tied, and my words get tangled.' Then the LORD asked Moses, 'Who makes a person's mouth? Who decides whether people speak or do not speak, hear or do not hear, see or do not see? Is it not I, the LORD? Now go! I will be with you as you speak, and I will instruct you in what to say.' But Moses again pleaded, 'LORD, please! Send anyone else.'"

What circumstances are you currently facing that you feel ill-equipped to handle? List your most common excuses for not fully surrendering to God's plan in these areas.

2 CORINTHIANS 3:4-6 (NASB)

"Such confidence we have through Christ toward God. Not that we are adequate in ourselves to consider anything as coming from ourselves, but our adequacy is from God, who also made us adequate as servants of a new covenant, not of the letter but of the Spirit; for the letter kills, but the Spirit gives life."

"The contrast here is between the law of Moses and the Holy Spirit, the primary features of the old and new covenants, respectively. The letter kills insofar as it pronounces judgment upon those who break the law. The Spirit gives life, because under the new covenant sins are forgiven and remembered no more, and people are enabled by the Spirit to live for God."[1]

ISAIAH 50:4-5 (NLT)

"The Sovereign LORD has given me his words
of wisdom, so that I know what to say to all these
weary ones. Morning by morning he wakens me
and opens my understanding to his will. The Sovereign
LORD has spoken to me, and I have listened.
I have not rebelled or turned away."

"Understanding is God-given perception of the nature and meaning of things, resulting in sound judgment and decision-making; in particular the ability to discern spiritual truth and to apply it to human disposition and conduct."[2]

JUDGES 6:14-16 (HCSB)

"The LORD turned to him and said, 'Go in the strength you have and deliver Israel from the power of Midian. Am I not sending you?' He said to Him, 'Please, LORD, how can I deliver Israel? Look, my family is the weakest in Manasseh, and I am the youngest in my father's house.' 'But I will be with you,' the LORD said to him. 'You will strike Midian down as if it were one man.'"

1 KINGS 17:8-16 (NASB)

"Then the word of the LORD came to him, saying, 'Arise, go to Zarephath, which belongs to Sidon, and stay there; behold, I have commanded a widow there to provide for you.' So he arose and went to Zarephath, and when he came to the gate of the city, behold, a widow was there gathering sticks; and he called to her and said, 'Please get me a little water in a jar, that I may drink.' As she was going to get it, he called to her and said, 'Please bring me a piece of bread in your hand.' But she said, 'As the LORD your God lives, I have no bread, only a handful of flour in the bowl and a little oil in the jar; and behold, I am gathering a few sticks that I may go in and prepare for me and my son, that we may eat it and die.' Then Elijah said to her, 'Do not fear; go, do as you have said, but make me a little bread cake from it first and bring it out to me, and afterward you may make one for yourself and for your son. For thus says the LORD God of Israel, "The bowl of flour shall not be exhausted, nor shall the jar of oil be empty, until the day that the LORD sends rain on the face of the earth."' So she went and did according to the word of Elijah, and she and he and her household ate for many days. The bowl of flour was not exhausted nor did the jar of oil become empty, according to the word of the LORD which He spoke through Elijah."

request if she'd known that her obedience to God's command would have resulted in such provision?

"Zarepeth" means "refinery" and is likened to a "workshop for the melting and refining of metals." It was a veritable furnace for men; a place of assay and refining both for the prophet and the widow with whom he lodged.[3] How do circumstances like what the widow experienced here refine us?

2 PETER 1:2-3 (AMP)

ay grace (God's favor) and peace (which is perfect

well-being, all necessary good, all spiritual prosperity,

and freedom from fears and agitating passions and

moral conflicts) be multiplied to you in [the full, personal,

precise, and correct] knowledge of God and of Jesus

our Lord. For His divine power has bestowed upon us all

things that [are requisite and suited] to life and godliness,

through the [full, personal] knowledge of Him Who called

us by and to His own glory and excellence (virtue)."

position

pore & paraphrase

pull

pose

plan

PSALM 84:11-12

"For the LORD God is a sun and shield; the LORD gives grace and glory; No good thing does He withhold to those who walk uprightly. O LORD of Hosts, how blessed is the man who trusts in You!" (NASB)

"For the LORD God is our sun and our shield. He gives us grace and glory. The LORD will withhold no good thing from those who do what is right. O LORD of Heaven's Armies, what joy for those who trust in you." (NLT)

Do you have a question about "God withholding no good thing"? At times in our lives this may seem false. All things that come to those who live righteously or according to his will are good things. What in your life makes this hard to believe?

Is there a "good thing" that it seems the Lord is withholding from you right now? In light of this passage, how should you adjust your thinking about the things you do have and the things you don't?

MATTHEW 14:15-20 (HCSB)

"When evening came, the disciples approached Him and said, 'This place is a wilderness, and it is already late. Send the crowds away so they can go into the villages and buy food for themselves.' 'They don't need to go away,' Jesus told them. 'You give them something to eat.' 'But we only have five loaves and two fish here,' they said to Him. 'Bring them here to Me,' He said. Then He commanded the crowds to sit down on the grass. He took the five loaves and the two fish, and looking up to heaven, He blessed them. He broke the loaves and gave them to the disciples, and the disciples gave them to the crowds. Everyone ate and was filled. Then they picked up 12 baskets full of leftover pieces!"

The standard Jewish loaf of bread provided a meal for three.

The disciples were to learn that "no situation appears to Him desperate, no crisis unmanageable." [4]

PHILIPPIANS 4:19

"And my God will supply all your needs according to His riches in glory in Christ Jesus." (NASB)

"And this same God who takes care of me will supply all your needs from his glorious riches, which have been given to us in Christ Jesus." (NLT)

position

pore & paraphrase

pull

pose

plan

Paul encouraged and applauded the generous giving of the believers at Philippi and promised that they could expect that God would meet their needs in return.

Note that the supply is not "out of" His riches but "according to" them. This means that what God supplies is in harmony with His glory and purposes and corresponds to it in its type and its extent.

HAGGAI 2:3-5,9 (HCSB)

The prophet Haggai to those rebuilding the temple

" 'Who is left among you who saw this house in its former glory? How does it look to you now? Doesn't it seem like nothing to you? Even so, be strong, Zerubbabel'—this is the LORD's declaration. 'Be strong, Joshua son of Jehozadak, high priest. Be strong, all you people of the land'—this is the LORD's declaration. 'Work! For I am with you'—the declaration of the LORD of Hosts. 'This is the promise I made to you when you came out of Egypt, and My Spirit is present among you; don't be afraid. ... The final glory of this house will be greater than the first,' says the LORD of Hosts. 'I will provide peace in this place'—this is the declaration of the LORD of Hosts."

position

pore & paraphrase

pull

pose

plan

The grand temple built by Solomon had been destroyed approximately 66 years before. Some may have recalled it from their childhood and could easily have seen that their current structure paled in comparison. Read more in 2 Chronicles 2–4.

Do you find yourself ever comparing your past to your present? How does the Lord's word to His people in Haggai 2:9 provide encouragement to you?

MORE SEEDS
Jeremiah 1:9; Matthew 10:19; Mark 13:11; Luke 12:12; Job 12:13; Proverbs 2:6;
1 Kings 4:29; Philippians 2:13-14; Psalm 84:11; 2 Chronicles 13:14-18

SESSION 3

FULLY
SURRENDERED

DVD SESSION: CONTROL

> "[Jesus] did not consi[der]
> with God as something
> for His own advantage."
> –Philippians 2:6, HCSB

Two thousand pounds.

That's how much he weighs. He's a well-kept, massive animal with a gorgeous coat that glistens like soft sequins when touched by sunlight. Accented by a long, jet-black mane, he draws the admiration of many. Every step reveals sinewy muscle that flexes with each move of his chestnut-colored body. The biggest of all the horses in the stable, he is indeed a sight to behold.

When he comes out into the open arena, it's common to hear someone catch his or her breath. He's immense, tall, and wide. His name is Goliath.

When my brother Anthony first laid eyes on him, he had to have him. A horse lover since he was a youngster, Anthony could only stare at this colossal creature and hope that he'd be able to take him home. After a bit of a negotiation, he found that he could.

. did.

When his prized animal stepped out of the trailer onto the new grounds that he'd now call home, my brother led him directly to the round pen. It's a small patch of bare ground about 60 feet in diameter outlined by a three-board wooden fence. Compared to the wide, open spaces where the horses run loose, it's tiny. It has to be because this pen is for training.

As beautiful as this horse was, he'd be useless, not to mention dangerous, unless he knew, understood, and complied with the pecking order in his new environment. In fact, his gargantuan size made this even more important. He could easily muscle his way out of any circumstance he wanted to (it's clear when you're standing next to him who has the upper hand), so a sense of compliance and a willingness to yield to his trainer was paramount.

I watched while Anthony trained. He stood in the center of the pen as the horse circled him, running around and around the edges of the ring. Finally, Anthony yelled "Whoa! Whoa!" The gallop slowed to a canter, then to a trot, and finally a walk. When cued, Goliath stopped abruptly, and Anthony worked to get him to turn his attention to the center of the ring and walk directly to his outstretched hand. He didn't get it at first ... or second or third.

For one full hour I stood on the outside of the round pen with my foot perched up on one of the wooden slats, elbows out, chin in my hand, resting on the top one, as they rhythmically went through this routine.

"It's critical," Anthony yelled over to me. "If we don't get this right, neither one of us will enjoy each other's company. If he doesn't learn to corral his strength, then he'll be too dangerous to ride. Learning to yield is paramount."

Corralling our strength
This exercise wasn't about stripping him of power but about teaching him to control it and yield to legitimate authority.

Yielding to authority.

These are hard notions to comprehend. Our human nature seems to demand the opposite. We yearn to use every bit of our potential whenever and however we choose.

We've grown to feel that this is our right: to assert ourselves at our own bidding. "Why else would we have been given the strength and potential that we have?" we reason to ourselves. And yet the One with all power in the palm of His hand seemed to live differently:

Though He was God, He did not think of equality with God as something to cling to. Instead, He gave up His divine privileges; He took the humble position of a slave and was born as a human being (see Phil. 2:6-7).

Can you imagine how much Jesus "weighed"—with all that influence, power, authority, majesty, honor, wisdom, and heavenly supremacy at His disposal? Yet the most powerful man of all gave up the right to utilize and flaunt that authority. He chose rather to submit to the will of His Father and to demonstrate His care to those He loved. He chose not to take full opportunity of the power that was rightfully His nor to override the authority of His Father's will. He did so in order that He might display to us a principle He knew full well would be a difficult yet necessary code for us to live by.

If He could willingly choose to submit to the will of His Father, which He knew would even include the most gruesome of all deaths, shouldn't we?

Every man and every woman

Every married couple and every single

Every employee and every boss

Every child and every parent

Every citizen and every governmental authority

Every congregant and every shepherd

No power worth flaunting and no authority worth usurping will give any of us the amount of satisfaction and enjoyment that comes from aligning with the divine design established by God before the foundation of the world. "It's critical," the Spirit whispers underneath the rebellious protests of the ever-changing cultural tide, "learning to yield is paramount."

Into the round pen of God's Word we go. Sure it seems a bit narrow compared to the wide, open spaces our culture stretches out before us to roam in. Yet the One who purchased us stands in the center. He calls men and women, young and old alike. No matter our power or strength or position, we can only experience freedom in His presence.

See His arm outstretched.

Hear His voice saying, "Come."

He'll teach us to have the same attitude that Christ Jesus had (Phil. 2:5-7) so we might reap the full enjoyment and benefit of lives well ordered and fully surrendered.

PHILIPPIANS 2:5-9 (AMP)

"Let this same attitude and purpose and [humble] mind be in you which was in Christ Jesus [Let Him be your example in humility:] Who, although being essentially one with God and in the form of God [possessing the fullness of the attributes which make God God], did not think this equality with God was a thing to be eagerly grasped or retained, But stripped Himself [of all privileges and rightful dignity], so as to assume the guise of a servant (slave), in that He became like men and was born a human being. And after He had appeared in human form, He abased and humbled Himself [still further] and carried His obedience to the extreme of death, even the death of the cross! Therefore [because He stooped so low] God has highly exalted Him and has freely bestowed on Him the name that is above every name."

*"As God, He [...]
all the rights [...]
yet during His i[...]
state He surrende[...]
right to manifest Hi[...]
visibly as the God of a[...]
splendor and glory."[1]*

*What does your
willingness to submit
reveal about your level of
humility?*

*Consider the confidence,
security, and strength
Christ must have had to
be willing to subject Himself to the circumstances
He endured. If you were
teaching this passage,
how would you explain
the connection between
a person's strength and
willingness to yield to
authority?*

position

pore & paraphrase

pull

pose

plan

(Christ) had
f deity, and
carnate
ed His
self

...ples on being a servant:

...mself and said, 'You know

...ne Gentiles lord it over them, and

...eir great men exercise authority over them. It is not

this way among you, but whoever wishes to become

great among you shall be your servant, and whoever

wishes to be first among you shall be your slave; just

as the Son of Man did not come to be served, but

to serve, and to give His life a ransom for many.' "

*"Exercise authority
refers to the exercise
political power but with
an implication of compul-
sion or oppression. In the
gentile world, ruling by
dominion and authoritari-
anism was common."*[2]

*"Greatness in the Lord's
kingdom does not come
through rulership or
authority but through
service (20:26-27). A
leader's goal should be
serving, not ruling."*[3]

1:7-8 (NASB)

to Joshua—Moses' successor

very courageous; be careful to do according to all the law which Moses My servant commanded you; do not turn from it to the right or to the left, so that you may have success wherever you go. This book of the law shall not depart from your mouth, but you shall meditate on it day and night, so that you may be careful to do according to all that is written in it; for then you will make your way prosperous, and then you will have success."

Joshua's success as a leader would be directly connected to His willingness to yield.

It is striking that God's instructions here to Joshua are not about military matters, given that Joshua and the Israelites faced many battles ahead. However, the keys to his success were spiritual—directly related to the degree of his obedience to God.

apernaum, a centurion came forward

ng to him, 'Lord, my servant is lying

paralyzed at home, suffering terribly.' And he said to him, 'I

will come and heal him.' But the centurion replied, 'Lord, I

am not worthy to have you come under my roof, but only

say the word, and my servant will be healed. For I too am

a man under authority, with soldiers under me. And I say

to one, "Go," and he goes, and to another, "Come," and

he comes, and to my servant, "Do this," and he does it.'

When Jesus heard this, he marveled and said to

those who followed him, 'Truly, I tell you, with

no one in Israel have I found such faith.' "

What does the insight the centurion expressed reveal about his view of authority and submission?

Note that those in authority should themselves be submitted to a higher authority.

ull
pose
plan

ive to your masters with all respect,

o are good and gentle, but also to

those who are unreasonable. For this finds favor, if for the

sake of conscience toward God a person bears up under

sorrows when suffering unjustly. For what credit is there

if, when you sin and are harshly treated, you endure it

with patience? But if when you do what is right and suffer

for it you patiently endure it, this finds favor with God."

How do you relate [to] those over you when [their] character or conduct is unreasonable? How might not only your behavior but also your disposition emulate Christ?

Authority is the right to act or speak in certain ways, in accordance with the authorization of a higher power. All human authority derives from God and is to be exercised in a responsible manner.

Note the Scripture is not commanding us to yield to abusive authority or authority that leads us into sin.

His arrest and crucifixion

...em, 'My soul is deeply grieved, to the point of death; remain here and keep watch with Me.' And He went a little beyond them, and fell on His face and prayed, saying, 'My Father, if it is possible, let this cup pass from Me; yet not as I will, but as You will.'"

"He (Jesus) pleaded for some other way, if God's purpose could allow it. This makes it all the more impressive that there was in the end no question that the Father's will had to take priority, whatever the cost."[4]

He was about to "drink the cup" that His Father had prepared for Him, and this meant bearing on His body the sins of the world (John 18:11; 1 Peter 2:24).[5]

In what circumstance are you finding it difficult to submit to the Father's will because of what doing so will cost you? How might God be glorified and others benefit from your obedience?

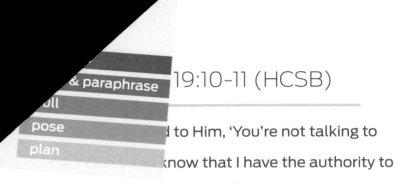

& paraphrase 19:10-11 (HCSB)

ull

pose

plan

...d to Him, 'You're not talking to ...know that I have the authority to release You and the authority to crucify You?' 'You would have no authority over Me at all,' Jesus answered him, 'if it hadn't been given you from above. This is why the one who handed Me over to you has the greater sin.'"

Even those in positions of the greatest authority have been given that authority and will be held accountable.

"Let every person be subject to the governing authorities. For there is no authority except by God's appointment, and the authorities that exist have been instituted by God" (Rom. 13:1, ESV).

How should knowing that leaders have delegated authority from God affect how you view and respond to their position?

ery human institution and authority

for the sake of the Lord, whether it be to the emperor

as supreme, or to governors as sent by him to bring

vengeance (punishment, justice) to those who do

wrong and to encourage those who do good service.

For it is God's will and intention that by doing right

[your good and honest lives] should silence (muzzle,

gag) the ignorant charges and ill-informed criticisms

of foolish persons. [Live] as free people, [yet] without

employing your freedom as a pretext for wickedness;

but [live at all times] as servants of God. Show

respect for all men [treat them honorably]. Love the

brotherhood (the Christian fraternity of which Christ

is the Head). Reverence God. Honor the emperor."

When the laws of governmental institutions contradict the teaching of Scripture, does this submission still apply? Read Acts 4:19. How might one still respond honorably to those in leadership?

...aders and submit to them, for they keep... ...ver your souls as those who will give an account, so that they can do this with joy and not with grief, for that would be unprofitable for you."

How can you begin submitting with "joy and not with grief"?

What do you think the author meant when he wrote "that would be unprofitable for you"?

In what current circumstance are you finding it difficult to submit to the Father's will because of what it will cost you?

2 KINGS 5:9-14 (NET)

"So Naaman came with his horses and chariots and stood in the doorway of Elisha's house. Elisha sent out a messenger who told him, 'Go and wash seven times in the Jordan; your skin will be restored and you will be healed.' Naaman went away angry. He said, 'Look, I thought for sure he would come out, stand there, invoke the name of the LORD his God, wave his hand over the area, and cure the skin disease. The rivers of Damascus, the Abana and Pharpar, are better than any of the waters of Israel! Could I not wash in them and be healed?' So he turned around and went away angry. His servants approached and said to him, 'O master, if the prophet had told you to do some difficult task, you would have been willing to do it. It seems you should be happy that he simply said, "Wash and you will be healed."' So he went down and dipped in the Jordan seven times, as the prophet had instructed. His skin became as smooth as a young child's and he was healed."

Like Namaan, do you doubt that your submission would have any effect or benefit on your current situation? What might this reveal about your character?

Has a lack of surrender ever kept you from God's best? Explain.

MORE SEEDS

God has ultimate authority. Proverbs 21:1; Job 23:13; Job 42:2; Psalm 135:6; Isaiah 14:27; Isaiah 45:9; 1 Corinthians 11:3; Daniel 2:21; Husband and wives: Ephesians 5:22,25,28,33; Colossians 3:18-19; 1 Peter3:7; Ephesians 5:25-29; Children and parents: Joshua 24:15; Ephesians 6:4; Genesis 18:19; Ephesians 6:2-3; Deuteronomy 5:16; John 5:19; Ephesians 5:21; Ephesians 1:22-23; 1 Corinthians 16:15-16; Jesus' example: John 13:4-15

LEADER GUIDE

Thank you for leading a Seed Bible study group. Here is some information you might find useful:

1. The two Seed studies include six Seed DVDs. Each contains a modern-day parable on video and a list of discussion questions. You can purchase them individually and use them to foster a one-time Bible study discussion or simply use the DVD presentation as an enhancement for an event or meeting.
2. For ongoing meetings, we've combined the DVDs into two packs—three in each pack. Each set covers three weeks of meetings. Seed Pack 1 and Seed Pack 2 both contain three video parables, each presenting a different theme, and one member book for the leader.
3. Individual members will need to purchase their own member book to enhance their participation in this study. Additionally, the books can be used without their accompanying DVD session for individuals or groups that prefer the print only.

At your first meeting explain:
1. This study is unlike others. Each week will present a different theme.

2. This study is designed to stimulate conversation with God through Scripture to become more personal and will be worth their effort. Some thoughts that I share in the introduction may help you with this.
3. Introduce the "5 P" method, using my description from pages 7-11. Familiarizing yourself with this process will help you explain it and answer any questions.

Watch the DVD and use the discussion questions to stir the conversation. Before you conclude your meeting, remind participants to use the "5 P" method to continue their conversation with God for the remainder of the week. Explain that there is no homework to finish or problems to solve—just Scripture to meditate on. Encourage them to select one passage each day. I've purposefully given more Scripture than necessary in hopes that this resource can be used again.

When your group reconvenes the following week, allot some time for members to share what they sensed the Lord saying to them from the passages they reviewed. After the designated time, watch the next video in the series and start the process for the following week. Thank you for your diligence in serving God's people. I am praying for you.

Blessings, Priscilla

FORGOTTEN

Background Scripture:
Matthew 6:25-34; Luke 12:4-8

1. What kind of circumstances cause you to feel forgotten?
2. How do you react when you feel overlooked?
3. How would people around you know you have felt forgotten?
4. Discuss Luke 12:7, "Indeed, the very hairs of your head are all numbered."
5. Where else in Scripture do you see the Lord showing that He cares for the "forgotten"?
6. What are some practical ways God's care has encouraged you when you feel like a fifth sparrow?
7. How would you explain how much God cares to someone who doesn't know Jesus?
8. Dig more into the context of Luke 12. In what personal ways do verses 22-30 speak to you about worry?
9. In what way have you overlooked someone lately? How can you be careful to cause this person to feel valued going forward?
10. You are valuable, but how do you show other people around you that they are valuable too?

ENOUGH

Background Scripture:
Psalm 84; Philippians 4

1. How many times a week do you worry about having enough?
2. What are the things you are most concerned about being deficient in?
3. What has your concern kept you from participating in?
4. What influences in your life prompt you to feel unsatisfied and to want more than what God provides for you?
5. What is on your wish list with God that He has not chosen to give you right now? Consider this in light of 2 Corinthians 12:9-10.
6. Read and discuss God's promise in Psalm 84:11. What about your life makes this easy or difficult to believe?
7. Why do you think we are all prone to worry? What practical steps can we take to more effectively obey Matthew 6:25-34?
8. In what ways does God supply all your needs (Phil. 4:19)? How does trust enter into this equation?
9. Paul didn't say God would supply all of my wants. How do you see the difference between wants and needs?
10. In what sense do you recognize "you have everything that you need"?

CONTROL

Background Scripture:
1 Corinthians 11:1-3

1. What feelings do the words *submission* and *control* conjure up for you?
2. What are some areas where you feel a compulsion to control when you are supposed to yield?
3. The need to control is often rooted in fear. What fears cause you to desire control?
4. Why do you think some of us feel more compelled than others to always be in control?
5. Why do we so often fight being under the control or authority of someone?
6. Submission to earthly authority is often an indicator of how we will submit to the Lord. What does your track record reveal?
7. If you are single, assess your relationship to those in authority over you. Do you follow them willingly? cheerfully? In your job or school, how does this apply?
8. If you are married, in what cases do you think a wife is not to submit to the leadership of her husband?
9. In what relationships do you need to relax and let someone else lead?
10. What may happen (good or bad) if you let someone else lead? What may happen (good or bad) if you refuse to let someone else lead?

11. How do you need to relinquish control of your relationship to God so He can steer instead of you?
12. What divinely given responsibilities are you neglecting because you are too busy controlling responsibilities He hasn't called you to?

ENDNOTES

Session 1

1. Warren W. Wiersbe, *Expository Outlines of the New Testament* (Colorado Springs, CO: Victor, 1992).

Session 2

1. D. A. Carson, *New Bible Commentary: 21st Century Edition* (Downers Grove, IL: InterVarsity Press, 1994).
2. W. Arndt, F. W. Danker, and W. Bauer, *A Greek-English Lexicon of the New Testament and Other Early Christian Literature* (Chicago, IL: University of Chicago Press, 2000), 795.
3. H. D. M. Spence-Jones, editor, *The Pulpit Commentary: 1 Kings* (Bellingham, WA: Logos Research Systems, Inc., 2004), 395.
4. Bruce Blomberg, *Matthew* (electronic ed.). Logos Library System; *The New American Commentary* (Nashville: Broadman & Holman Publishers, 2001), 232.

Session 3

1. John F. Walvoord, Roy B. Zuck, *The Bible Knowledge Commentary: An Exposition of the Scriptures* (Wheaton, IL: Victor Books, 1983), 654.
2. Gerhard Kittel, Gerhard Friedrich, Geoffrey William Bromiley, *Theological Dictionary of the New Testament* (Grand Rapids, MI: William B. Eerdmans, 1995), 240.
3. John F. Walvoord, Roy B. Zuck, *The Bible Knowledge Commentary: An Exposition of the Scriptures* (Wheaton, IL: Victor Books, 1983), 66.
4. D. A. Carson, *New Bible Commentary: 21st Century Edition* (Downers Grove, IL: InterVarsity Press, 1994).
5. Warren W. Wiersbe, *The Bible Exposition Commentary* (Wheaton, IL: Victor Books, 1996).

WITH WORSHIP BY ANTHONY EVANS

PRISCILLA SHIRER

DON'T MISS THIS INTIMATE & INSPIRING EVENT!

lifeway.com/goingbeyond | 800.254.2022

Event subject to change without notice.

LifeWay | Women